GRAVITY IN ACTION ROLLER COASTERS!

Joan Newton

The Rosen Publishing Group's
PowerKids Press™
New York

Published in 2009 by The Rosen Publishing Group, Inc.
29 East 21st Street, New York, NY 10010

Book Design: Michael J. Flynn

Photo Credits: Cover © vasile tiplea/Shutterstock; p. 4 © MaleWitch/Shutterstock; p. 4 (beach ball) © Christophe Testi/Shutterstock; p. 5 © suravid/Shutterstock; p. 6 © Cary Kalscheuer/Shutterstock; pp. 9, 10 © Historical Picture Archive/Corbis; p. 13 © marotta michele/Shutterstock; p. 14 (top left) © Xavier Domenech/Shutterstock; p. 14 (top right) © Douglas Greenwald/Shutterstock; p. 14 (middle right) © Abramova Kseniya/Shutterstock; p. 14 (middle left) © Eric Isselée/Shutterstock; p. 14 (bottom left and right) © Morgan Lane Photography/Shutterstock; p. 17 http://upload.wikimedia.org/wikipedia/commons/5/55/PKDHypersonicDrop.jpg; p. 18 © David C. Rehner/Shutterstock; p. 20 http://upload.wikimedia.org/wikipedia/commons/c/c5/Steel_dragon_2000.jpg; p. 21 http://upload.wikimedia.org/wikipedia/commons/c/ca/Kingda_Ka.jpg; p. 22 © Kazuhiro Nogi/AFP/Getty Images.

Library of Congress Cataloging-in-Publication Data

Newton, Joan.
  Gravity in action : roller coasters! / Joan Newton.
      p. cm. — (Real life readers)
  Includes index.
  ISBN: 978-1-4358-0008-3
  6-pack ISBN: 978-1-4358-0010-6
  ISBN 978-1-4358-2976-3 (hardcover)
  1. Gravity—Juvenile literature. 2. Force and energy—Juvenile literature. 3. Motion—Juvenile literature. 4. Roller coasters—Juvenile literature. I. Title.
  QC178.N49 2009
  531'.14—dc22

                                    2008036792

Manufactured in the United States of America

CPSIA Compliance Information: Batch #CRO16250PK: For Further Information Contact Rosen Publishing, New York, New York at 1-800-237-9932

CONTENTS

GRAVITY IN ACTION

Gravity is a force that acts on all matter on Earth. It pulls all objects toward the center of Earth. Gravity is what keeps everything from floating into space!

We can't see gravity, but we can see its effect. When you jump into the air, gravity pulls you back to the ground. When you throw a ball, it curves toward the ground and comes down. When an apple falls from a tree, it drops to the ground. When you pour liquid into a glass, it flows down, not up. These are examples of gravity in action!

What other examples of gravity in action can you think of?

What happens when you throw an object?

4

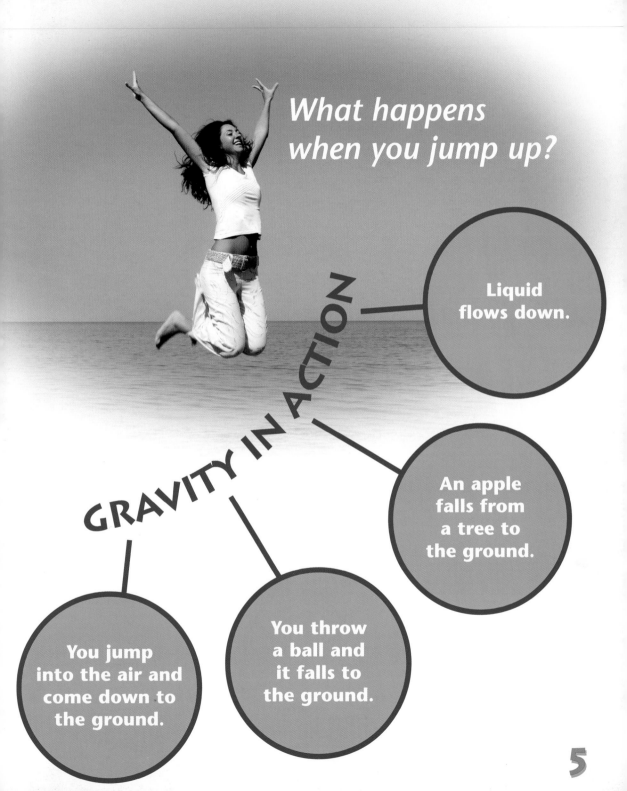

What happens
when you jump up?

GRAVITY IN ACTION

Liquid
flows down.

An apple
falls from
a tree to
the ground.

You jump
into the air and
come down to
the ground.

You throw
a ball and
it falls to
the ground.

5

ROLLER COASTERS

Have you ever been to an **amusement park**? Have you seen a roller coaster? Maybe you've even ridden one.

What do you know about roller coasters? Many people think they're **exciting** rides. When did people first ride them? What kind of power keeps a roller coaster moving? Do roller coasters have their own power? Do you wonder how coasters that twist and turn can be safe? Do you know which coaster is the highest? Are you curious about what makes some roller coasters faster than others?

In this book, we'll learn the answers to these questions as well as other interesting facts about roller coasters.

Many roller coasters have hills and curves. Have you ever been on a roller coaster like this one?

THE FIRST ROLLER COASTERS

Maybe you've sledded down a hill on a snowy winter day. For centuries, people have had fun sliding down hills of ice and snow on boards or sleds. Did you know that gravity is what pulls sleds down snowy hills?

In the 1400s, man-made hills—covered with snow and ice—became popular in Russia. People climbed a ladder or stairs to the top, then slid down very fast. These popular slides were called Russian Mountains.

In the early 1800s, people who lived in places that weren't as cold as Russia copied the idea. At first, they built and waxed long, steep wooden hills. Then, they used wheeled cars on tracks. Before long, someone had the idea to join the cars together.

These were the first roller coasters!

This painting shows a crowd gathered to ride and watch the fun at a Russian Mountain.

9

10

The first coaster in the United States originally had a useful purpose. It was a train that was built in the 1800s to carry coal down a mountain. Mules pulled the train cars up the mountain. At the top, the coal and mules were loaded onto the train for the ride down. The force of gravity moved the train down the mountain. A worker who operated a brake stopped the train at the bottom.

Many people came to see the gravity railroad work. After the train was no longer needed to move coal, it took people for exciting rides down the mountain.

Other people began using gravity trains. Before long, a machine system was built to pull cars back up the mountain.

This is a painting of the train that was the first American coaster. How is it different from roller coasters you've seen or ridden?

STORED ENERGY CHANGING TO WORKING ENERGY

STORED ENERGY	WORKING ENERGY

roller coaster at the top of a hill

roller coaster moving down the hill

horse standing

horse jumping

runners at the starting line

runners racing

Energy is everywhere. We use energy every day. A roller coaster uses two kinds of energy—stored energy and working energy. Stored energy is the energy an object has when it's still. Working energy is the energy an object has when it's in motion.

A coaster at the top of the first hill has stored energy. Gravity pulls it down, setting it in motion. This changes the stored energy to working energy.

As the coaster comes down the hill, it goes faster. This gives it energy to move up the next hill. The force of gravity then pulls it down that hill. Throughout the ride, gravity changes the kind of energy the coaster has and keeps it in motion!

These pictures show the difference between stored energy and working energy. What examples of stored and working energy can you think of?

LAUNCHING COASTERS

Many people enjoy riding roller coasters. They like the speed and want to ride coasters that are higher, faster, and longer. So, people who build roller coasters try many different ways to make the ride more exciting.

We've already named some kinds of power used to move coasters up the first hill. Coaster builders are always looking for ways that are faster than pulling coasters uphill. Today, some coasters are **launched** by the force of water, air, or **electromagnets**.

Launched coasters use working energy quickly. If a coaster doesn't get the speed it needs on the first launch, it can sometimes be launched again. Some riders hope this happens—they want to go backward on the track and speed forward again!

This was the first coaster that was launched using forced air. It was sent very quickly almost straight up!

The practice of launching roller coasters has added a great deal of speed to roller-coaster rides. Today, coaster builders also include many twists, turns, and **loops** to make the ride even more exciting. Some coasters have more than one train running on the track at a time. Some coasters even spin the seats as the coaster twists and turns on the track!

To keep roller-coaster rides safe as well as exciting, computer systems are used. Most systems separate the coaster track into blocks. In each block, the speed and motion of the coaster can be controlled. Computer systems also control the way riders are secured in the seats.

These riders stand throughout the ride as the roller coaster loops and turns upside down. They are secured by a shoulder frame that keeps them in place.

KINGDA KA

RECORD-BREAKING COASTERS

People who plan, build, and ride roller coasters know which are the fastest, tallest, and longest.

As of 2008, the world's fastest and tallest roller coaster was in the United States. The Kingda Ka is a rocket coaster. It can go 128 miles (206 km) per hour! Its highest point is 456 feet (139 m).

The world's longest roller coaster is in Japan. It's called the Steel Dragon and is more than 1 mile (1.6 km) long!

STEEL DRAGON

A BIG THRILL

Many roller-coaster riders think that turning upside down is the most **thrilling** part of a coaster ride. For these people, a roller coaster in Japan is the best. It turns its riders upside down fourteen times!

Roller coasters have changed in many ways since the first coaster was built, but they still use gravity to work. If you could plan a roller coaster, what would you include to make the ride exciting?

GLOSSARY

amusement park (uh-MYOOZ-muhnt PARK) A park with different kinds of rides.

electromagnet (ih-lehk-troh-MAG-nuht) A magnet wrapped in wire through which an electric current is passed.

energy (EH-nuhr-jee) Usable power.

exciting (ihk-SY-ting) Causing fear and other strong feelings.

gravity (GRA-vuh-tee) The natural force that causes objects to move toward the center of Earth.

launch (LAWNCH) To throw forward.

loop (LOOP) A circle or oval that stands on its edge.

motor (MOH-turh) A machine that produces motion.

thrilling (THRIHL-ing) Causing an exciting feeling.

INDEX

Due to the changing nature of Internet links, The Rosen Publishing Group, Inc., has developed an online list of Web sites related to the subject of this book. This site is updated regularly. Please use this link to access the list: http://www.rcbmlinks.com/rlr/rlcst